The Real Warnings

ANHINGA PRESS

The Real Warnings

Rhett Iseman Trull

RHETT ISEMAN TRULL

for Coventry, my sister in poetry. With good wishes for your own writing & with gratitude,

Rhett

2008 Anhinga Prize for Poetry

Selected by
Sheryl St. Germain

ANHINGA PRESS
TALLAHASSEE, FLORIDA 2009

Cover art: *I Stopped in at the Farmhouse,* oil on canvas by Dan Rhett, 2006
Author photograph: Jeff Trull
Design, production, and cover design: C.L. Knight
Typesetting: Jill Runyan
Type Styles: titles and text set in Perpetua

Library of Congress Cataloging-in-Publication Data
The Real Warnings by Rhett Iseman Trull — First Edition
ISBN — 978-1-934695-11-1
Library of Congress Cataloging Card Number — 2009929754

This publication is sponsored in part by a grant
from the Florida Department of State,
Division of Cultural Affairs, and the Florida Arts Council.

Anhinga Press Inc. is a nonprofit corporation dedicated wholly to the publication
and appreciation of fine poetry and other literary genres.

For personal orders, catalogs
and information write to:
Anhinga Press
P.O. Box 10595
Tallahassee, Florida 32302
Web site: www.anhinga.org
E-mail: info@anhinga.org

Published in the United States
by Anhinga Press
Tallahassee, Florida
First Edition, 2009

For Mama, Daddy, and Jim
&
For Jeff, always

Contents

Acknowledgments

I offer grateful acknowledgment to the editors of the publications in which the following poems, some in slightly different forms, first appeared or are forthcoming:

The American Poetry Journal: "Girls Who Will Never Be Prom Queens," "Signs," and "The Streets of My Heart"

The American Poetry Review: "Introducing My Brother in the Role of Clark Kent"

The Bat City Review: "Talking All Day to the Dead"

The Comstock Review: "Old Dog"

Explorations: "The Real Warnings Are Always Too Late"

The Greensboro Review: "Instructions on How to Leave Me"

The Hampden-Sydney Poetry Review: "Playing Games"

Iron Horse Literary Review: "Last Word," "Nobody's Goddess," "This Poem Is Begging for Help"

Kakalak: "To My Student, Struggling"

LiturgicalCredo: "Counting Miracles" (as "Counting Miracles at the State Asylum")

Poet Lore: "The Ice Is Our Only Light"

Prairie Schooner: "Can I Hold It?" and "The Night before Depakote"

roger: "Dim Rooms They Call Dark," "Lovers on a Walk," and "To Find Her True Love, the Gardener of the Orchard Turns to Magic"

Runes: "The Bells in My Skin Still Ring"

storySouth: "Everything from That Point On," "The Last Good Dream," and "Solitaire"

Unmoveable Feast: "The End of the Hour," "Extinct Means Once They Ruled the Earth," "The House of Pain," "Secrets the Whales Wish They Didn't Know," "Sonogram on the Way to Earth"

Waccamaw: "Naming the Baby for Mark and Terra," "Well before the Party Started"

Yemassee: "The Lion Doesn't Live Here"

Zone3: "Borderline, Promiscuous"

"Counting Miracles" appeared in *After Shocks: the Poetry of Recovery for Life-Shattering Events.*

"Everything from That Point On" appeared in *Best New Poets 2008.*

"The Real Warnings Are Always Too Late" won the *Explorations* Award from the University of Alaska Southeast.

"Signs" won the Noel Callow Award from the Academy of American Poets and the University of North Carolina at Greensboro.

"Heart by Heart the House," "Lovers on a Walk, "Sonogram on the Way to Earth," and "Study of Motion" won awards from the Dorothy Sargent Rosenberg Foundation.

My thanks to the Dorothy Sargent Rosenberg Foundation, *Explorations* and the University of Alaska Southeast, the University of North Carolina at Greensboro, and the Vermont College Postgraduate Writers' Conference for fellowships/scholarships and prizes that supported and encouraged me during the writing of this book.

I am grateful to my teachers for their generous guidance and insight: Fred Chappell, Lucille Clifton, Stuart Dischell, Christine Garren, and Deborah Pope. Thanks also to my fellow students at the University of North Carolina at Greensboro's MFA program, who helped shape many of these poems; and to Dan Albergotti, Tom Christopher, Angie DeCola, Gail Peck, Nina Riggs, Melissa Tarleton, and Roger Weingarten for their careful reading and advice.

To Sheryl St. Germain for selecting this book and to Rick Campbell, Lynne Knight, and everyone at Anhinga for their time, talents, and support — my endless thanks.

Finally, I wish to thank my family for their encouragement, inspiration, and support, without which this book would not be possible. And to Jeff, my best friend and closest reader, I offer my deepest gratitude and love beyond words.

The Real Warnings

The Real Warnings Are Always Too Late

I want to go back to the winter I was born and warn you
that I will flood through your life like acid
and you will burn yourselves on me.
On my sixteenth birthday, I will use the candles
to set the basement aflame and run out laughing,
wearing smoke like a new dress. With a pocket knife,
I will try to root out that life you so eagerly started.
I'll dent the garage door with my head, siphon Crown Royal
from your liquor cabinet, jump from a gondola in Venice. I'll smash
my ankle with a hammer, drive through stop signs
with my eyes closed, cost you thousands
in medical bills. Forget about sleeping.
I'll dominate the prayers you keep sending up
like the last of flares from an island no one visits.
For every greeting card poem, I will write four
to hurt you. Some will be true.
Other people's lives will look perfect
as you search the house for its sharper pieces.
And when they lock me up I'll tell the walls
I'm sorry. But these warnings will come like candles
after a night of pyres. I already know
how you will take one look at that new life screaming
into the world, and open your arms,
thinking, if it looks this innocent,
it cannot be so bad.

The Last Good Dream

Dusk and the two of us again
on the porch swing, idling down
the day. The low sun burning out

but still with us, its full glow
like the lull between seasons
or the soft pearl of the oyster.

It is the moment when doves
light on dormant phone lines and boys
find love in fish nets and crab cages,

in the salty chorus of the wharf. We
can almost hear them, six blocks east,
the lobstermen bringing in the catch

and their daughters in braids telling secrets,
a cloister of curls and intentions, waiting
for fathers whose bones smell of fish

to carry them home. By habit
our arms touch as we listen to the cadence
of the first evening rain tapping to the west

near the cemetery and the eight-stool pub.
A girl coasts her bike down the street,
bells on her handlebars ringing. It is the hour

before women wash dishes
and men go out, before the gulls flock
toward Captain's Calabash, the shore's single light

for miles. And we give
with unthinned hearts, little knowing
how, even if banked by the best words

and buoyed by honesty, love can fail.
Or maybe we do know
and unharbor ourselves anyway.

Introducing My Brother in the Role of Clark Kent

My brother tells me the story of Lois, the secrets
glinting in her eyes like kryptonite, her broken steps
and sharp elbows on the dance floor, the other women
in their bed from time to time. On ecstasy
her sophomore year, they said *I love you* for the first time
and he held her, felt like Superman, even
when she woke up screaming
from a dream she wouldn't speak.

Tonight he repeats word for word her bad jokes; the recipes
for her invented snacks like peanuts soaked in Jack
and chocolate-coated; names she called him in the dark
as their cigarettes died out beneath the wild ghost
their mingled smoke had formed. *Like a flower
in negative light,* he says. *That's how it looked,
that beautiful.* And I wonder if he's high. I don't
interrupt. This is the most he's talked to me in years
and I'm aware of the possibility
he's forgotten I'm here on the other end
of this line that's become his confessional. Besides,

he's not asking forgiveness or even if he was right to leave
her after three years, after trying to live
together and apart, trying sex sober
and drunk and hand-cuffed, after memorizing
her cousins' names and which foods she hates
and which rides to avoid at a fair. He took the drugs, too,
slept on the floors of strangers, carried her home
hungover, her arms clinging around his neck, her body
trembling like a meteor crashing through

the atmosphere. This has always been
my brother's role: hero

not quite strong enough. His first lead was Seymour
in his high school's production of *Little Shop of Horrors*, prior
to his growth spurt and Osgood-Schlatter,
years before his biceps bloomed. Knobby knees buckling,
he carried his Audrey twelve steps across the stage, delivered her
to her doom, knowing the irony, knowing
that in the audience all three nights were other women
he couldn't save: his mother who wanted
divorce, who grabbed his hand weeping in the mall
last week, praying aloud right there
in the middle of the crowds; and his sister
they call clinically depressed, suicidal, though he tries
to explain that's not possible,
they don't know her, weren't there
when she was young and told him all
her secrets, all her dreams, leaping from the bed
in her Wonder Woman underwear.

As for Lois, he's calculated that he's spent
seventy-one-point-two percent of the last three years in her
presence, mostly happy, unwilling to trade a day of it, not even
that last evening by the statue in the park, as the carriages
trotted past on their ceaseless circuitous route
and my brother finally managed a goodbye,
staring at her sweater's neck, at the loose string
he no longer felt the right or duty to mend,
Like the string of a balloon I was letting go, he says,
up into the sky where I can't follow anymore.
And when she left the park alone, he bought himself
a carriage ride, wrapped around him like a cape the blanket
beneath which how many thousands of men had closed their eyes
and held onto their women?

The Boy in the Full-Length Women's Fur Coat

He lives in New York City, rides
the L train late — it's almost
empty — thinks of her,

the girl he keeps loving
and losing, the girl who sleeps alone
tonight, somewhere in the Carolinas

where the stars have almost emptied the sky
of black. She must love him still,
the way last night's dreams

linger in the morning's mood. She must
love him despite his wandering.
The L pulls late into Union Square.

His date gave up, went on without him
to the bar whose name he can't remember.
The sky is a black laugh above him,

driving down its rain. The city's lights
skate the puddles like fallen fireworks. No one
to shine on, to turn on.

He remembers the night
the dunes caught fire. It was July 4th
at Emerald Isle. And she was scared, the girl

he keeps loving, whose name,
on his tongue, means hunger. Scared
in her sundress and yellow

hair ribbon, she let him skate
his fingers around her naked
ankles. He tries

to prefer these city girls with their
piercings, their way of staring hard
into the light like statues, these dates

who go on without him,
give up, despite his biceps, his spiky hair.
For awhile he shone on, turned on, as always,

not even missing the tick of the rain
through leaves, the shutters and kickplates
of suburbs. Or her, the girl whose dreams

lingered behind his every move
once upon a time for a year or two.
He lights a cigarette

just to be holding something. Strangers
pass, faces half-hidden by scarves.
Maybe he will follow one, sit beside her

on the L. Late, when it's almost empty.
Arm around her just to be holding
a stranger, who will leave. And he'll shudder,

loving her still, the girl left behind in her
one-stoplight town that's lost
its mystery yet still goes on

when the streets have emptied
and even the strays
have fallen asleep with their hunger.

Solitaire

He has learned to love the loneliness of night,

The possible hauntings, faraway sirens, the silver
Of the sky. He used to follow all the advice: hot baths, warm milk,

Soft jazz, no caffeine. He tried sleeping with socks and without,
In silk or cotton sheets. He even took pills, which made him feel
Upon waking, as if he'd slept through a play's second act.

He would rather let the rare half-hour naps come when they will:
After a midnight plate of celery sticks and peanut butter, perhaps,
Or in the middle of a cricket serenade
Accompanied by dogs barking across their fences.

He's never tired, but he can't help feeling left out,
As if he's the punch line to night's only joke, as if the dreams
He could be having are piling up like unclaimed luggage.
By four a.m. even his west coast friends are asleep. He turns
His clocks to the wall. He dances in the empty

Street, swings upside-down from the trees.
He rescued a kitten, named her Lady, likes to watch her sleep
On his windowsill or curled up purring in his popcorn bowl.
He croons Elvis into the handle of his garden spade
While standing on his coffee table, dressed in tails. He juggles,
Stitches, makes categorized alphabetized lists of the movies he's seen,

Books he's read, each pet he's owned from Amadeus to Zephyr.
But mostly he plays solitaire. Decks of cards, stacked in multiples of five,
Rise like towers of miniature cities in the corners of his apartment.
His goal: to collect enough to play with a new deck
Every night for the rest of his life, however many that may be.

He tries to welcome them, to imagine them being dealt out:
New stars turning over beside each fat ace of a moon.

Nobody's Goddess

The fat girl at the bus stop who bleaches
her mustache and still wears jelly shoes
that went out of style years ago, pretends
as the other middle-schoolers snicker
at her yellow slicker and closed umbrella
slung like a rifle over her shoulder.
She pretends the rain has just begun and she alone
is protected, all the other girls trying to hide
their see-through blouses, perms frizzing,
the boys inching away for fear of static
shock. They come to her
for shelter, call her smart — no,
ingenious — for always thinking ahead.

On the bus they will vie to sit by her,
in the back, the popular section. And anyone
who dares throw pencil stubs in her direction
will have to contend with her new defenders.
With admirable humility she'll protest
the attention, the friends suddenly
everywhere, bearing love notes and roller-skating
party invitations. She will list what in the past
worked against her: straight A's,
teacher's pet, no fashion sense, and
of course, the non-symmetrics of her face.

But that's why we love you, they will say.
Your face is puckered like the sea, the thick
lenses of your glasses greenly glowing
when the science lab is dark: burners on.
We watch you for the formulas.
You're a goddess we've misunderstood. But now
we know: the split ends of your hair are wishbones;

your freckles, cities on a map. Please condescend
to come to the cool girls' slumber parties.
Allow the cutest boys to walk you home. Please
let us hang our dreams on the hook
of your nose. Let us launch our hopes
behind the talisman of your unibrow.

Naming the Baby for Mark and Terra

Call him Granite, Argonaut, Thievery-Slick. Tusk
or Wolfe with an "e." Call him Steel and dream him tougher
than the names kids fling at each other. What about Thor?
Can't you just picture him mjolniring down the football field,
the other team parting like the sea for the divine? Give him
a name like Mahogany Foxx, a name that looks good
in calligraphy. Will he be famous? Will he fly rockets?
Will he dance like rapids on a river? Name him River.
He may paint, sail, fight to save endangered antbirds of Brazil.
Will his be a quiet life of books and coffee? Or
a black-ops in the jungle life? Or both? Anything
is possible for Thunder/Claw/Cathedral/Wing. Imagine:
how many letters he'll sign *Love, Avalanche*; how many hours
he'll spend in the Atlantic, in museums, in the back of the line
because, like his father, he's the tallest.

Go to Aladdin's Castle in Roanoke ten years from today.
In the high score columns of which games
blink the initials *PWT*? Phoenix Wildebeest Trull.
Listen to the roar in twenty-two years
when Mercury Flyer takes the stage, electric guitar
over his shoulder, sparkly indigo pick in his teeth. Hey!
What about Sparkly Indigo? No, make that Indigo Spark.
Nothing like a unique moniker to get the world to chin-up
and notice. Don't get mad. Please, don't take offense.
I know how serious a task it is to give the baby this first gift.
You want to get it right. The perfect name,
followed by exposure to Mozart and Moses and Beatrix Potter,
vegetables and violin and no films rated R. Of course,

as soon as he adventures out of the womb, he belongs to the world,
to its swindle and swoon, its crow and cringe,
where you can't protect him with a name, you know.

All kids are going to get beat up in some way over something.
At least give him a name he alone can claim as he tumbles
into the fray. I have wishes for him, too.
He will be my first nephew, a golden crown
that he should feel upon him from the start, his name glinting
among the Mikes and Christophers. Now is your chance
to anchor him to earth (Greenery, Stone) and launch him
into flight (Albatross, Krypton). Call him
something royal: Duke or Kingfish. Something inscrutable
like Mist. Call him Ghost that he may linger.
Let his name be Arrow. Let it startle, when spoken,
the bow of the mighty tongue.

To Find Her True Love, the Gardener
of the Orchard Turns to Magic

I have cast a love spell and am waiting
for the night to web itself with signs:
>   the rosy wreath around the moon,
>   the plumped spiders bellying up,
>   glow-worms on the cider tanks,
>   and bourbon on the bull's breath.

I have waited years for love to cast its own spell, for you
to run your thumbs along the straps of your overalls
and ask, *What about it? Why don't we?* But
my hair is graying at the temples
and my best friend's youngest daughter
is engaged to the boy who used to clean the stables
on his summer break. Love. What is it
but protection from being a wallflower
or being seated between strangers on a plane?
What is it but a variation in the picture albums?
An excuse to pin on any emotion, like a perennial
insisting its way through each season?
Maybe my true love doesn't
>   write letters to prisoners every Sunday,
>   name his dogs after Roman gods,
>   sing the blues while scrambling eggs,
>   or drive his pick-up with the windows always down.
But it would be nice. It would be nice if suddenly
the slow ticking of your pulse sped up
when I walked by and you began to realize
>   why I always call you when the termites return
>   or when I need help with a dress that buttons up the back,
>   and why, through cracked knuckles and finicky mistresses,
>   I've stayed on here all these years.

Oh, you blind fool man with your dimples
and scrapbooks, I give you up. The spell
is cast. The love stone is in my belt even now,
knocking against the spade. I'm leaving the matter
to magic, which is already filtering out
the usual misdirections, honing the needle of time to avoid
what would have been more waste.
Soon there will be no more featureless days,
no finishing off the apple pie alone.
Already every face I come across
seems like an offering. Why, just today there was
        the salesman at Lowe's with his fertilizer discounts,
        the painter with the dragonfly tattoo,
        that mousy delivery boy now suddenly exotic,
        and you coming in from the orchard, still oblivious,

still everything I want.

Lovers on a Walk

for Sarah and Christian

Electric down the avenue, they spark us
        as they pass. Street lamps pop, a tire swing
                spins like a yo-yo letting out. Their stop and go
        is a discotheque in Florence, their to and fro a night swim,
naked. Sprinkler heads rise
        like a chorus line lifting its hats, time zones shift, the tide
                swindles free of the moon. Their laughter's
        as sure as a sawed-off muffler. Their whisper
is a corset untying. Phone lines cross like puppet strings tangling,
        someone drops a china plate, a widow returns
                to her V-necked reds. Bark peels, satellites blink,
        ants carry their queen to a new hill.
She is his country, he is her map. Stars
        jump from their constellations, mist touches down
                in the desert, every clam in Charleston unhinges.
        They are a Russian ballet, a rock 'n' roll ballad, a book
we cannot put down. All the fireflies glow at once,
        a riderless bike switches gears, cats and dogs follow them like
                a piper. But they don't even notice our uncoverings, our
        salutings. Or that behind them, the rain has begun to hiss
on pavement still warm in the wake of their desire.
        When they do look up to see the world, they will find us
                tigered and jazzed, played as we are
        by their brass band love. They will find us hauntingly beautiful,
bent as we are in the lens of their passion.

Lotion Cigarettes Candles Wine

From your kitchen spills her difficult laughter, another
manipulation to draw you in. And sure enough, you leave me
on the couch, go to listen to the story
she'll punctuate, as always, with complaint.
I follow you to her and linger at the table,
straightening the knives on the napkins.

She's beautiful. I, too, was charmed
the moment I saw her. I clung to her friendship, her
smiles like fine china. I took her authority
for wisdom and never saw coming:
Who had the most warping childhood? Who is best
acquainted with death? With passion? With you?

As she spices the chicken parmesan, you slip
your fingers through her belt loops, kiss the corner
of her mouth and tell her she tastes like peppermint.
Already, I'm thinking ahead
to my long walk home past the streetlight
where you once waited for me
with a bag of pistachios and a block
of cheddar, promising
we'd stay up all night on the balcony
practicing guitar chords, watching for comets,

not knowing I am dangerous at midnight
when I'm lonely and I glimpse
your chest hair peeking
from your collar, not knowing
how often I imagine the click of your teeth
against mine. Or how often I accidentally love.

I suppose she's the better choice. She cooks you
healthy dinners, gives the best back massage.
She's read more books and had more sex than I.
She's thinner with longer eyelashes and always wins
Trivial Pursuit. Even the contents of her freezer,
scallops and coffee beans, speak of sophistication. I study
the only lessons left for me: her voice
on your answering machine, her lipstick staining
your favorite mugs, her handwriting on your grocery list:
Lotion Cigarettes Candles Wine.

Playing Games

At first my love for you was safe, unopened.
Just the two of us rolling the dice, timer
still in its box. Lying on opposite ends
of the game board, imagining smiles
on the monstrous faces of every
dust mite between us. Imagining
the letters in your tray: *B E R C U H L*
almost *Hercules*, almost *be cruel*.
I loved your receding hairline, fuzzy pink slippers,
your castle of mason jars waiting
for bugs. And the science in your head always
excited: drums of the cerebellum, choir of
ions serenading every synapse. What if

we'd kissed, what if we'd said, *I love you*
in my body's five imaginary time zones,
I love you roller skating, I love you
in my dreams when you save me
from the vampires? I can hear it now:
the minor chords with the bright orange flash
of *G A M E O V E R.*
We decided instead to be logical,
to wait until we're sure we won't hurt
each other, as if the scorecards will never fill,
as if the planets of our neuroses
might one day actually align. Meanwhile

we date who comes along with a swing
of her hip or his collar turned up:
the woman who ate all the brie
at Victor's party, the new guy at Starbucks
who dollops whipped cream on my frappacinos.
We've agreed this is our best move, holding

until all chips are in.
I'm the first to worry. You've been busy
on the beach without me, skipping your heart
across the water, examining
shells where creatures used to live.

Everything from That Point On

I.
All day the gulls dove, cries unsynchronized,
throats clinching every note as tightly as their bills

pincered quivering fish. The morning wind, spiked
with salt, stung our eyes as the sun slashed its light

across the numb horizon. *I guess this is mine now,* you said,
by default, drumming your chewed fingernails

with a hollow *ruc-a-tuc, ruc-a-tuc* on the bumper
of your father's truck, our reflection skewed in its dents.

And everything from that point on was slow motion:
the rest of the day spreading between us without words,

sunbathers coming and going, building their castles
until the tide slithered in to crush the towers in its grip.

Then the cooler air, clouds wisping thin, the last
of the fishermen reeling in, and the loon on one leg

letting the pink wings of sunset molest her feather by feather.

II.
Alone, under the cold fist of the moon and backed by hazy winks
of distant hotel lights, you slogged in calf-deep, the waves

gutting the ocean floor, sloshing its dregs against
you. From the shore I memorized

each splintered shell, each man-of-war, each muscle
you didn't flinch. Without ceremony, you slung the urn

out past the breakers, its lid tipping, dark tail of ashes
trailing. As you returned, the chill of the night

trembling through you, the smell of the brine in your hair,
I knew this would be the end for us. Your green eyes were pale,

scaled of their usual laughter. You swung from your loss,
gills straining. I loved you most in that moment, knowing

even as I slipped my arm up the back of your shirt, hooking us
together, that you were about to cut me loose to spare me

the tightening of the line, the bruise of sudden air.

This Poem Is Begging for Help

The first line's okay, that rain-soaked Labrador
drawing you in right away with his patient eyes.
You can't help feeling sorry for the little guy (whose tag
reads *Skywalker*) when you picture him waiting
at the front door of the gone-to-bed house,
the house where his boy lives, where his boy sleeps now
with cold feet, having kicked off the *Star Wars* bedsheets
in a fevered fit. You love this dog

as he cocks his head, ears faithfully alert,
listening for the creak of footsteps on the stairs, the turn
of the lock. Surely soon he'll hear strong running
and it will belong to his boy. But here in stanza two
you start to get antsy. You just can't help it.
Why isn't anyone coming for the dog? It's not right
to leave him in the cold night where the wind blows the rain
into needles. You want answers. You want to know

why there is a soccer ball going flat
under the azaleas. That must be in the poem
for a reason. But when more clues are dropped in
and the dog slumps to the stony ground with his head
on his paws, everything cries revision: the sweaty
nightshirt, the *Get Well* cards taped to the boy's walls
like cave hieroglyphics, and in the yard the sigh of the dog
who knows only that he's never been left out before.

Each time the lights go on upstairs, he is up
and wagging, ready to sleep at the foot of the bed,
his boy toeing his ears, whispering his name in the dark.
Come morning, they can play ball again. He'll even pretend
to be a horse. His boy likes that game. He barks
an eager hope, but no one opens the door. You knew

it would happen this way, knew it would end with your wish
for amendment, for some way to fix

this dangling last line, this waiting dog's wet whine.

Signs

for Harry Lee

Today has been hollowed out by your death
like a thrown-away fruit rind rotting in the fairgrounds
in the off season, between a gum wrapper and a torn ticket,
beside what used to be The Ghost Train.

The sky is the color of dirty rain, and nothing
flies in it. Skeletal trees rasp their limbs together
like a witch's ready fingers. And I am glad.
What I can't say, the tipped-over shopping cart outside Wal-Mart

says for me. And the hub cap rusting in the ditch grass, the bent
candy-cane decoration losing its grip on the streetlight
downtown. *The world is a tied-on fender*, you once said,
then winked, *But the rope is strong.* When the doctors

moved you from home, your lawn was kept mowed,
and even now someone remembers to plug in your tree, the one
your best friend strung with three thousand lights
while your lungs worked against your bucking heart.

Tonight: no moon, no stars. I never realized before
how noisy the planets are. I praise their choice
to be absent. I praise the protruding ribs
of the stray ducking under the crawl space. For I know

there will come a day when the trees
are a kelly green belly-laugh in a sugared breeze, dogs
with meaty voices will frisk under a rekindled moon,
and I'll fall asleep without tears, traitor to my grief.

Talking All Day to the Dead

The cake keeps falling. No wonder with the music so loud, so loud
the pictures shake.

Gotta wear a hat. It's cold and the dog goes out, comes in, goes out.

The women. The women are softening.

Except for Sarah.

Freezing rain tonight.

Flowers by the guard rail. D in Algebra.

Remember when we came here with the feathers and the wine?
It snowed all day. And you with the holes in your gloves.

Why can't I sleep in my car forever?

Everyone in tonight.

Except for Sarah.

Sleet is punching holes in the leaves.

Gotta drag Sarah back to the house. She hates, loves, hates you.

Stereo blasting song
to song. The dog's water would tremble if his bowl wasn't empty.

If We Still Believed the World Was Flat

Instead of tending
    to my children's runny noses
        and letting out my husband's waistband,
            I would find a boat, cobalt blue, the color of rest, and

slowly,
like a barnacled beast who knows nothing
but to go, to go, to lay eggs
and abandon her nest
to the wet noses
of curious
dogs,

        I would sail with eyes cool
           upon the horizon, tight as an empty
               clothesline; and beyond, the nothingness
                  dark as the house-grave of the loggerhead

who lugs
her carapace shaggy with sea-moss
and would go far, so far,
in order
never to
come
back.

Study of Motion

City after city. After awhile all the rooftops
            and industrial plants and baseballs next to gutters
                        are the same.
                                    After awhile
                        you forget where you first tasted s'mores,
where you slept the worst, where you earned nicknames
                        you've left behind. *Little Cricket*:
                                    who called you that?
You've forgotten the streets
            where the filling stations stayed open all night.
                        Weren't there always small cafés
                        and fields of horses just outside of town,
            where every woman walking her dog was an important part
            of your education, your study of motion:
                        how loneliness feels good
                        sometimes, how walking away
                                    is nevertheless stepping forward?

            Hanna, drawing chalk poinsettias on the sidewalk,
                        once said, *Pursue Joy Now* and sounded solid,
                                    like the TV emergency signal.
                        You get the feeling she fears nothing,
            which can't be true, but it's nice to believe,
                                    especially now that you're alone
                        on the side of the road, engine still, no white towel
                        tied to the mirror.
            Ducks skid, landing on the lake behind you,
                        the lake the city dug when it cut the highway through.
Some boys in a convertible whistle as they pass
            and it's almost enough
                        to be noticed by fleeting strangers, to be
                                    waiting for a storm or a ranger signaling
            from the fire tower across the bypass.

It's almost enough to know
           that Hanna, twelve years your senior,
        is moving to San Francisco; with wind in her hair
           she will do what she loves.

           You wonder, in the day's late light,
                       how many more cities
        you'll sleep, rent, believe in
                   before you fall into a final love,
     sign a final contract, lock the door behind you
           and never make it home.
                   It's the sound of sirens that prompts you
        to get off the side of the road
     back into traffic,
               to smooth the creases of the map and join
        the flatbed trucks, the horses' tails
           swishing through the slits of trailers,
               the station wagons hauling their families
                       before a banner of exhaust.

The Ice Is Our Only Light

Naming the details of winter won't help you
when you show up without a coat

and sit in the hallway outside my apartment,
not bothering to knock. A neighbor has to call

to warn me *that strange girl is here again*,
before I open the door to your slippery eyes,

always bluer than last time. You say nothing.
You crawl inside, curl up on the carpet,

letting the cats venture to study your damp hair.
And what can I say? You know about

the buried blades of grass, the squirrels
glad their foraging paid off. The power's out again

and the south doesn't have enough snowplows.
There's nowhere to go on a night like this.

I could say *be strong* but what does that mean?
You do what you must to carry on.

Like Sisyphus talking to his rock:
When we get to the top, you'll fly away.

He gives his rock a new name for every journey.
And you've got your tricks, too. Who am I

to offer advice or throw out careless words
like *wrong* or *danger*? I'm just the old friend

who's witnessed years of breakdown
after breakdown: alcohol and Xanax binges,

scars hidden under bathingsuit straps.
I can't tell you anything about pain

you don't already know: how sooner
or later you'll wake to find your burdens

shifting. Food will again have taste, your hands
will work your body, coaxing pleasure out.

You know what feels like the end is the end
only if you pull the trigger, which is why you're here

to be watched like a prisoner, like a ghost
of questionable intent. Good choices are trying

to cling to you. So am I, beside you under the blankets
as the wind picks up. Deep in the cold earth

the moles huddle together. Another branch
snaps under the ice. Morning is on its way, yes,

but first the dark must darken.

The House of Pain

*I never yet heard of a useless thing that was not ground out of existence
by evolution sooner or later. Did you? And pain gets needless.*
— H.G. Wells, *The Island of Dr. Moreau*

There is a bell on the gate but it does not ring.
The cat on the porch is dead. He wears
no crown of blood. No scent marks the air
as witness that life once pounced here.
Even the maggots refuse to jewel him.

None of this surprises you as you try the door,
which opens easily enough without a lock.
The room, as expected, is windowless, white.
Echoes would stick to the walls if you spoke,
though even the clocks do soundless work,
their strict hands
                                wheeling on.
You lie down where broken eggshells hide
the cracks that fork the floor. Inside you,
Dr. Loneliness picks up his merry scalpel
and you forget the lick of your name
across the board of chalk. Gone the graffiti
of childhood. Gone the wish lists and the whirling
glass bottle.
                        But you often remember
the cat on the porch and you wonder
if anyone's come to bury him. The thought
of the breeze having its way with his whiskers
and snowflakes settling between the pads
of his untwitching paw, is almost enough
to move you. But the numbness
has been spinning your bones into silk.
You're asleep in the hull of yourself.

Pity the man who comes in after you,
the man who loves your stale bread heart.
Like a paramedic with his first D.O.A.,
he is sure he can save you.
So you undress for him, whisper
what he wants to hear, calculate your
quick breath and your little candied noises.
But he knows that, to you, his tongue is a dangling rag,
his fingertips a swarm of gnats trying to stir

the stagnant water.
As he drags you by your hair
toward the radiator, swearing you will feel it
this time, a wonderful fear opens its wings inside you
and gratitude splays you out,

awakened. As you leave, what begins to haunt you
is not the blisters that bangle your wrist like opals.
It is not the awful things he did to you
but the *yes* that you roared as you let him.
You will learn to loathe and love
the *yes* that saves you
and the bell on the gate that never
rings and over the cat —
your step
again.

Rescuing Princess Zelda

for K and N

I. CHECKING IN

False certitude hovers over everyone. Even the doctor keeps
clearing his throat, looking away. His face should
sour in my direction, a textbook list of labels
glittering his sentences. Not this kindness
that feels like a trick. He whispers to the nurses and
their smiles drip like watercolors in rain.

I want to hear what he said. I want their hair in tight buns.
Nothing is as I imagined. The orderly's telling a joke, steam
rises off the lunch trays. I'm listening for muffled
screams that never come. In the movies there's always
some rubber-room borderline waking
the ward because she can't find her red shoes.

But these halls are quiet webs of shadow, light. Only
as my father walks my mother away,
only as I imagine them holding on to each other
all night in a house that will feel too big, do I see myself:
delicate but not yet blurred, and I think,
You bird-boned fool, what have you agreed to?

II. NIGHT ONE, ADOLESCENT WING

My head sings to itself like a horror
movie score: half
lullaby, half devilhum.

hush little baby don't say a word

The heat struggles on, dies off. I'm too
hot. But I want the sheets covering
my feet. Suffer. Repeat.
Shouldn't be here. Really.

My friends must be out
perching on bar stools. My friends
in their tight pants and glittery make-
up, insisting nothing
is mis-webbed about me. But

if everything I did was for the chance
to be caged, lie
still, de-perfect,

if that mockingbird don't sing

then what about the details
I never told anyone, performances
to an empty house: the curling
iron held out the window
into the rain, me thinking *sacrifice;* cigarette
lighter opening my skin
in secret circles, red
and itchy as thought; my soccer

trophy — *Most Valuable* — buried
in the dunes where, nights earlier,
I invited a stranger to slip,
as if lifting a wallet
off an ignorant mark, his tongue
inside me.

III. WHY VOLUNTEERS AREN'T ALLOWED TO GIVE LAST NAMES

Last year Josh had a crush
on a girl from Duke who, to earn credit
for her abnormal psych class, visited
every week. During rec hour, with her
roommate, she made the rounds, lingering at the game
station or the art table for watercolors and origami. This girl
could fold paper birds with wings that really
flapped. She told Josh stories about her
classes, her brother in the army. Only five years
older than Josh, she confessed she, too, wanted
to kill herself once — in high school when she hurt
her knee and couldn't head
the cheerleaders anymore, and then
her father left. When he got out last
December, Josh rode the bus to Durham, found her
in the Duke directory, carried
roses to her dorm. She'd already
gone for the holidays, home.
Her roommate looked as if
she were face to face with an escaped
con. She kept the chain
on the door. Next thing
Josh knew, the hospital called
his house, accusing. And his stepmom said,
yeah, he'd been acting
not quite right. When they checked him
back in, he decided he'd give them crazy. Now
he kicks at nurses, tips over lunch trays, refuses
to do anything at rec time except
play Nintendo, rescuing
Princess Zelda.

IV. BORDERLINE, PROMISCUOUS

Each night when the ward closes into shadow,
when the only sounds are doors opening distantly
and footsteps of the evening staff who live between
our world and that other I've almost forgotten,

May waits until she thinks I'm asleep, then begins
her fluttery sobs. No one would guess this
is the same May who struts around all day
in shirts ripped off at the midriff, who flings
her long flamingo legs over the side
of the rec room's single arm-chair and tells us
adventures from her life before, stories we pretend
to believe just to keep her talking, laughing, head tilted
on that pale slender neck. We don't care

what the warnings say: *borderline, promiscuous*. May's quest
is our happiness. She's in love with us all.
Hands in the hair of the saddest, she works
the smile back out, until the nurses
intercede. For May, we break the rules.
Everything's red carpet and applause.
And should she choose to whisper a secret
to some lonely one of us, that lucky soul is king
or queen of the day. Or in my case,

the night. After the meds and first bed-checks,
during the song of the pipes, I lie still,
barely breathing, falling asleep
to the wild tears of May taking flight.

V. THE JUMPER

When good behavior earns him the right,
Casey's allowed to play his guitar, which is otherwise
locked in the nurses' station
because of the strings. Estelle, who works
nights, Wednesday through Saturday, lets him play
whenever he wants. He reminds her
of her son who's grown now and gone
somewhere, faraway.

In six years Casey will be out and dead.
I'll have almost forgotten him
when his face appears, framed
in the corner of the TV screen
on the five o'clock news, the anchorwoman,
pasty with make-up, announcing: *Police tried
to talk the jumper down, but ...*
And I will drop the dinner plate
and my young husband will rise, asking, *What?
Do you know him?*

I'll say no. The Casey I know is forever fourteen,
playing guitar for those of us with scars
across our wrists, beginning to puff
at the edges. The Casey I know leans over
the nurses' station to smile at Estelle
and croon, as if it's a love song:
*Be kind to your web-footed friends,
for a duck may be somebody's mother.*
He's got beautiful calluses written
on his fingers, and I'm one of the fans
imagining he will leave this place to become

a rock star. We crowd around him
as he strums our sad songs: industrial hum
of the lights, girls too thin to cast shadows,
grilles on the windows slicing the moon.

VI. DIM ROOMS THEY CALL DARK

If sleeps finds me, it keeps me
        floating on its surface, goose to be
startled — by anything dimpling the water (rain, fallen
                limbs) — into flight. The filtered darkness,
rooms lit enough for nurses
        to row gently among us adjusting
dosage, blurs the boundary between dusk and dawn, montage
              of memory catching in the web of dream:

Midnight. Snow hushes the avenue, mine
        the only prints as sadness escorts me
to the park, ice embracing the chains of the swing and the howl,
            in the woods, of the wolf who used to be

A man, swears Abigail, *is all we need*
        to save us. We're in fifth grade, the eve
of our first boy-girl party. When her hips split the seams
            of my miniskirt, I should warn — years of
starving that soon will divide
        her, us — I should deliver her
soup that comes steaming, quartets
        of cheese, blueberry muffins with

Frosting the windows, this weather contains us,
        me and the boy I'm kissing between
Luigi's House of Pie deliveries. When I open
            my eyes, his Pontiac's wheels let go. I'll be
blamed for his coma, I know (the crows
        down from the cedars already, devouring
           anchovies), I'll be locked in

A room full of birds. My piano teacher's house. Lake
            drained outside. Pale line around her finger where a ring
used to be. *Staccato,* she urges, *like this: pep-pe-ro-ni-piz-za.*
            I say no, not until she opens the cages.

VII. COUNTING MIRACLES

Some nights, Estelle lets us join her outside
while she takes a smoking break
and calls her girlfriend on her cell phone. Josh and May
and I sit nearby in the grass, leaning
against each other, counting miracles. Not
white doves drifting by at just the right moment
or some former comatose staggering back from the brink,
making talk-show claims about light. We don't believe
anymore in that rare luck some call blessing.
But we've learned a thing or two
about miracles for the common man,
the stuck man: a nest of robins about to hatch;
fast cars on the highway, going somewhere;
in the sky, webs of lightning. And that squirm of rhythm
whenever the stars flare up, holding on
to centuries of wishes, polishing them over
and over. The stars know the danger
of even a bingo-paced Wednesday and light
themselves every night in celebration
of the simple fact of our survival.

VIII. THE END OF THE HOUR

Out this window the finch, dulled
of gold for the winter, has found the feeder
empty. They are keeping my watch
in an envelope, sealed
until it's determined I'm safe
enough to let go. I tell time by the lengthening
shadow, the only clock in the room
facing the doctor who's been assigned
me. I like her. May says I'm lucky, the good ones
never last long here where the state
pays minimal and the furnace stinks
and the lights in the hallway flicker, fail.

My doctor is young, hasn't yet
heard it all, keeps meticulous notes as if
she'll be tested on this, on me.
When I puzzle her, wrinkles divide
her forehead, her fist grips, more
tightly, the pencil. Does she fear I might
lunge, attack? I'd never. In math, the compass
needle; in shop, the saw's teeth; all blades, always,
I've pointed toward me. It's the

end of the hour — for her, the end
of her day here. Where will she go? A movie?
A fiancé awaits. I can tell by the diamond
alone on her finger. Does she
let him know about me? Does she give me
an alias? May and I name her fiancé
Ernesto. We pretend to be them: she hides
nothing from him; he kisses her everywhere: the bed

47

of each nail, the valley where her voice
lives in her throat. We can't wait to be loved

like that, relieved of secrets
we keep for the protection of others. The hour's over.
Today's final question: not why
the scars but where? *Where else*
did you do that? She can't even name it.
And she doesn't mean
the woods by the park, the football bleachers, the arcade
in the mall with its jukebox of pinball and gunfire
punctuating an artificial dark. I
start to remove my blouse, to offer
a look at the marks I scored
that no one's ever seen. For a moment
I feel human, all masks put away. I will show
her all of it, ugliness I've covered until now, but
That's enough, she scolds, jotting a furious
phrase in her notes before opening the cabinet
with her heel and storing, again, my file.
Without looking up, she takes
one last sip of cold coffee, returns
the mug to the desk stained with so many rings
for so many years, a coaster
is pointless.
        Don't ask, I think, *if you don't want to know.*
But I say, *I'm sorry*, sorry familiar
as breath, *Sorry,* sent out the door half-
unbuttoned.

IX. CHECKING OUT

there are fewer words
now that i am a ball hog
without a ball, a foot
that leaves no print,
now that i dance
with my buck-toothed cousin
while my would-be lover winks at me
from the corner, tips
his wine glass, and whispers
to other girls. i am a road
with new speedbumps, a lesson
repeating itself a hundred times
on the blackboard. i am
the store-brand discount,
the ironed curls, and the extra
with no lines whose name
is left out of the credits.

The Night before Depakote

It's enough that we live, my old friend
and I. It's enough that we sit together,
lungs keeping duty, laughter now and then
taking its shortcuts through us. Tonight
is our first movie fest since
college and details split us,
since her apprenticeship to liquor
and my attempts to peel my skin off
like dried glue, get a good look at my bones.

We're watching a movie called *Beautiful Girls*.
There is ice on a lake, and I wonder
can water feel itself freezing? Do the fish
want to stay underneath forever?
A girl in the movie loves an older man.
They can't be together. We envy
their love-story pain, recollecting
spring afternoons before soccer practice
when we'd explore the empty
church on Ardmore, pretending
to be spies. I code-named her Stealth
because she was best at silencing her cleats
in the echo-heavy halls. We were unprepared
for the scenes ahead — eulogies, police —
walking the long way around to avoid
one another, our forgivable wandering
into different shades of the dark.

But tonight we're as close as always.
Closer. She's the same beneath
her sadness she won't betray

just to please an audience, as if she spent years
drawing her smile up from a well and now
wears it only when she means it. But who am I
on the eve of the whitewash?
Who will I be in the poemless country
to come? *I feel the words clot already,*
I tell her, *like salmon refusing to run.*
And my friend whose father is one-year dead,
whose mother was locked up for crazy,
my friend who will always
call me Dagger, takes my hands. *I don't care*
about your writing. I'd rather have you,
she says, as if the two were separate, as if
what kills one could save the other.

The Bells in My Skin Still Ring

Jim dares me to touch the wire that runs along the horse fence,
and staring into the stallion's wizard eyes, I do. Every wild thing
of the field perks up to sing in my orchestra.
I conduct the cricket strings, the horse hoof percussion.

When I come to, flat on the path, Jim is bent
above me, terrified his sister's been electrocuted. And he, too,
becomes part of the music, the moment surging through us,
his eye like the Magic-Eye, the Cat-Eye, hot green
with the signal's strength. Something inside each of us

must sense the changes, the curse taking shape: *bipolar.*
Next year I'll try my own cures, diagram my suicide
down the margin of my physics notes,
trajectory and *weight of gravity* invoked like magic spells.

And in the long season of pills and silence to follow,
we'll look back to this day as a lesson in the power
we hold over each other.
Jim, exhausted by cautious speech,
will lock himself up and swallow the key like Houdini.
And I'll soon forget the language of the stars,
the anthem of the beasts.

But right now heat from the pavement ignites
the fuse of my spine, my palms throbbing like a metronome
where they held, so briefly, the electric wand
of the fence. Jim stops asking if I am alive.
He steps back. Each blade of grass tenses beside his sneakers
as a mare in the field leans low with her blue whistle.

The Lion Doesn't Live Here

The lion doesn't live here anymore, his mane a fire trembling,
nostrils flaring every time the doorbell rings. The lion doesn't sing
in bass vibrato in the shower where fur still clogs the drain
and wet paws print the floor, though the lion doesn't live here anymore.
The lion doesn't drag me into spring's first rain
and make me dance the stalked-bird dance
for all the neighbors to see. The street is quiet now
except for suddenly fearless squirrels,
tossing acorns from the penthouses of their trees.
The only other play is gentle play: Mother-May-I,
pattycake, hopscotch and double-dutch. Yesterday I heard them cheer,
those girls with bouncy ponytails:

> *Where'd that lion go, I said, where'd that lion go?*
> *I don't care and I don't know. What?*
> *I don't care. He's long gone now*
> *with his crooked teeth and his velvet growl*
> *and his wicked head hung low.*

The silent moon of winter is a lazy oracle.
I ask why. She says,

> *you must forget*
> > *the click of his claws*
> > > *on the hardwood floor*
> > *and then you'll know.*

Meanwhile, salesmen return unafraid. And mice
in the walls retune their instruments. Their jazz concerts
shake the family picture frames as did the lion's roar
when he paced these halls before, but it's not the same.
I search the closets and attic to be sure, thinking maybe
goodbye was just another game. Maybe he'll sneak up purring
from behind the kitchen door and he'll laugh
that red hot laugh, cinders catching in his mane. But no,
the lion doesn't live here anymore.

Taking Rich for His AIDS Test

First the new sunglasses: expensive, sleek.
And I'm well aware of the glances we draw,
shopping on Melrose: Rich, the handsome could-be
movie star, and me —
his five-foot-tall sidekick wearing no lipstick.
He stops to appraise his reflection
in a Starbucks window, noticing the boy
behind the counter and, as always,
being noticed in return. He talks about his latest
date, some guy from Crunch,
says he should find a new gym with fewer
mirrors. But he knows he won't.
Over lunch, Rich says I'm good for him. I make him
less cynical. Then we leave a big tip, head for my car.
Already the afternoon light is changing.
I try to match his quick pace
past the fruit stand with its overpriced dates
where the vendor sweeps at shards of glass,
lodging them deeper into cracks of the sidewalk.

On the drive to the clinic, Rich drains of sarcasm.
Quiet in the passenger seat, he's nothing
but himself, which seems unnatural: a prowling
cat that's been belled, a sun eclipsing.

But first the new shades
to replace the ones the muggers stole.
He chooses mirrored lenses. Then a trendy
lunch that tastes like grass. And the cherry
lips of the waitress, the frosted tips of her hair, her
obvious disapproval of my sneakers. Can she look at me
and tell I'm a virgin?
Rich promises there's nothing wrong

with me, that when the right guy comes along I'll stop
being afraid. He says, *Your problem is*
you're taking sex too seriously.
And once again I'm wishing Rich
would leap across the table, sweep me into his arms
like a proper leading man, and make love to me
all night. It would be an initiation, nothing
more. An empty avenue, no
window displays, no browsing. Just two
friends alone among the starry glass
embedded in the sidewalk, lit by broken light.

Picked Up at a Party by Superman's Super-Hearing

Oh, sure, he's Superman *tonight*,
flying in to showcase, to grin with those
never-needed-braces teeth. Look at him posing
akimbo by the balcony door, which he's opened
just so we can all admire
how his cape
whips
in the wind.

Come on. I'll introduce you
if we can squeeze in through the mob. Yes,
there's always a mob. I mean, the man *is* brilliant.
He can calculate — *in his head* — the angular momentum
of a spinning object
while melting ice with his eyes
and, of course,
flying.

But last night I was with him on the roof —
yes, *with* him — and there was no pelvic supernova,
no exponentially-orgasmic-potentially-fatal
bliss. Trust me, hon, when it comes
to what matters,
flyboy's
just a man
after all.

Well before the Party Started

I was drunk, boiling over on the sidewalk, the blood in my brain aquiver,
a tuning fork. I was all bull's-eye and I knew it but joined you
anyway. Sure enough, my words broke leash and chased
themselves around the room. The looks on your faces
came flying, darts that should have hushed me
right away. But no, all my pockets had
split their seams at once, and there
went years of my loose change
rolling across the floor.

dear writer's guild   hello again
in your vast metropolis of glass of paper-clipped white light
again i am writing   from the tunnel
where dark water licks my ankles tries to turn my skin to scales
perhaps my last three letters did not make it
(increased surveillance
everywhere i go every alley bit by shadow
every old man with a cane ironically sprite of eye) if however
you have received my pleas i stress again how risky they are to send
how desperately i await your justice
as hollywood continues to incorporate my life into movies
without my consent   someone has been stealing my details
such as my scar from the buick my plastic barrettes
and my dreams always my dreams
i cannot hide i am continually plagiarized by exploiters
by hook-handed swindlers
who look like my father to confuse me
whose interpretations systematically slander me
as being a fatty or an invalid
some of the more obvious pilfering examples are as follows
teen wolf because i have an animal sense of the moon
karate kid makes unlicensed use of my fighting style
anything starring matt damon because he looks like me
and is cast accordingly   in order to portray me
as a janitor or murderer for blackmail purposes   the show friends
because i had friends in new york who were like warm pizza
until they were gone taken gone   homeward bound
because someone keeps snatching my pets
and they are trying to get back to me i know it
also a river runs through it because of the whole fish thing
there are more but i am out of room at any rate
the above should be sufficient for the guild to intervene

assign blame isn't that what you do
aim your gunnel cannons at the pirates please
do not call me at home   send someone in person
i know you know where to find me

.

Can I Hold It?

They look at each other first,
as if I might break it,
as if I might feel
how deep its ears go
or try to peel its eye
like a scab, as if I would think
of forcing its lids open, pinching
its nose closed, feeding it dirt, or worse —
messing with the boy part.
As if I might be wondering
where can I hide it,
what would the cat do,
if it will float. *Can I hold it?*
And this time they let me,
smiling, handing down
its open face, soft head,
no teeth for biting back.

There Was a Moment on the Way Home
When Hansel Left Gretel

Why, now that the woods are thinning, familiar again,
do you rush ahead, with only the occassional look back
to mark your progress by the distance between us?
Is it because this time I'm the one who led us
out of danger? At home when I used to cry you awake,
you'd trade your pillow for my damp one. You were boldened
in your boyhood. You were heroed: winning

each neighborhood wheelbarrow race,
venturing into woods to be nearer the wild,
telling me stories of our real mother, young
and beautiful. On clear nights, as we slept outside, watching
the stars glaze into morning, you'd say, *She must be*
up there, keeping her bright eyes on us. But the deeper

we wandered into shapeless woods, the less comfort
you could offer, no longer wanting me
at your side to witness how hysteria starts:
the purple lapse of hours, the hairy breath of panic. You gnawed
at the trees. *They will tell me where to go*, you promised,
your teeth full of bark. You cursed the birds,
stalked them with stones in your fists, even the blackbird
who led us to the house of butterscotch doorknobs,
licorice fringe on the drapes. We both believed

you could save us from anything, but in that cage
you screamed until your voice broke.
I'm the one who has killed for us, who still hears
the witch's bones snapping in the fire. I let you out
and led us as far as the lake. I'm sorry I tied you to the duck.
I know you don't trust birds, but there was no other way
to cross. I've seen you stopping

at each knothole to leave the ravens, as if paying
for protection, some of the witch's rubies.
I've been following this crimson trail, retrieving
our treasure. Please slow down,

come back. I miss your stories. I miss the sound of your steps
beside mine, crackling the leaves. I know fear
has braided your love for me with anger. I'm sorry
for the reminder, the remainder I am.
But don't you see? There's no getting away.
We are closer than ever, bound
by the parts of our story we can never tell.
I, too, heard the witch crying in her sleep
for the children stolen from her
when she was young and beautiful. I, too, know
that birdsong translates to lost in the forest's black fist
of a heart, where the trees cling close,
hiding the sky, erasing every star.

Old Dog

It was the day I learned that even a little girl
can give love away, can
put her fingers through the cage,
promise to come back,
and not come back. I still think of you

on these evenings, by the last of the glowing embers,
how your face was as centering as the sun,
your girl-laugh a spitfire in shadows.
Oh, and your pigtails bouncing! The secret tears
with me alone, the chapters you'd read aloud
after dinner with your fingers in my fur, the raw salt taste
when I'd lick your skinned knees.
In winter our sled rides, the wind
flapping my ears back; and watching
spring birds together.
Let's remember only
the pitch and chase of childhood,
your skip and my wag. Not the anti-climax

of goodbye. Not the fact that I grow old
without you. Let's refuse to think
of what's been lost: forgotten
bones in your old yard that will never be unburied.
And ah! the way you must look in lipstick.

I will always be yours, for you were the first
to say *good boy* and kiss the tips of my ears.
You were the burning wick of my best fortune.
And though I was still young when you left that day,
your face pressed like a wet leaf

against the back windshield,
though I was still young and new children
were waiting to call me another name,
my soul was already old with love. My heart
knew all its tricks.

To My Student, Struggling

for Johnnyke

The numbers just don't add up, I know. The answer
to *x minus y* is as hard to find as *sky minus moon, summer
minus iced tea*. You used to be able to navigate
days like these. You chased your brothers
through the woods, then caught the biggest fish.
But now you're between trains A and B
and one is sure to hit you. How to make sense
of it all — the crickets' voices in high octave,
the sweat stains and goodbyes — we're all
trying to figure it out. Sunshine buries her hands
in a box of marbles, steelies and cat's eyes
smooth against her wrists.
Haley checks herself into another hospital
where everyone's a fraction. And you,
stuck here in summer school, staring out the window.
You feel like the only one in charge of measuring
the universe. You feel stranded
on top of the mountain with no shoes, no horse,
no sled. The slow walk down has your ankles throbbing
before you take even one step. But somewhere below,
you've been promised, there exists a field of reasons,
and in it a lake of understanding. One swim
and you will know everything: the length
of the flagpole's shadow at noon, and how congruent
is your sectored heart. The fish in the lake
will nibble the blisters right off your sore feet
as their brothers whisper in your ears
wonderful, magical words like *isosceles, equality, right.*

Extinct Means Once They Ruled the Earth

We used to know the words to unlock each other,
even after mortgages, even after a season of endless
Little League games. We could make any hard day brighter.
I want to keep believing in the heat, in those backyard nights
when you called my heart a bird and traced my ribs for hours
under stars whose light meant they died long ago, long before us.

But today, as you come out of the bedroom, bags packed,
looking away, I can tell you are voiceless and would be cool
to the touch. Not even the sun can reach you and your Listerine breath,
your pulse the quick flick of a lizard's tongue.
The two hundred dollars you've left
is still on the counter under the dinosaur paperweight
Elliot made in Vacation Bible School last month.
What does extinct mean? he asked, in your arms.
And you said, *It means there are none anymore,*
but seeing his sadness, added, *Once they were everywhere,*
big as dragons, ruling the earth.

I don't ask where you'll sleep, what you will tell them
at the office, or how many pairs of socks
you've taken. My tongue is like a stubborn fly
buzzing against the back of my teeth, but I don't open.
I don't let the light in. And now you're really leaving,
careful not to step on the bald patch of lawn
where the fertilizer's still seeping in. You're wearing the tie
I gave you for Christmas, undone around your neck.
I meant to say something unforgettable. I meant to fix you
one last lunch with the apple pre-sliced
the way you like it. Your car door sounds
like the burp of Tupperware, shutting in its leftovers.
Your tail lights are the soft red sighs between us.

The cat and I watch from the window you recently glazed.
I wonder if she will miss nuzzling your rough cheek.
And Elliot. How long before he runs to the door
each time a car growls by? How long before he stops?
The world is changing and only the crows seem to know it,
along the picket fence, cawing their flint hearts out.
Meanwhile, the mailman is skipping our house,
the Taylor twins are rollerblading down our empty driveway.
It's August, the hottest day of the year. Strike
a match in this drought, and the hosta is bound
to catch fire. But it's January in my bones.
There's frost on my teeth. My ribs are a rattling glass cage.

Your Dear John

FADE IN to flashback, the kind blur of hindsight: curtains drawn
in your house in Burbank. Two screenwriters watching *Casablanca*,
cuddled close. I joke that my Dear John letter will be better than Ilsa's,
as across my lips, you play the petals of the red rose
you bought but say you

CUT. TO-

day, four months and three thousand miles later
I'm working on that letter when yours arrives, words like angry bees
in an uncovered nest. Your hair in a tANGLE, ON
you write, bent over your desk,
listing my wrongs with your best pen. At last,
this could be your blockbuster: *The Bad Girlfriend*. Draft two,
you'll make 120 pages, brads spearing the top and bottom
like brass stingers. But what will you include in your

MONTAGE SEQUENCE?
I stop the Writer's Guild elevator with my foot to let you in.
    You say, *Please tell me that's not a wedding ring.*
All those perfect lines you think up the night before, such as,
    on the windy Third Street Promenade: *I like it when you're tousled.*
And me the perfect audience: spec scripts and no agent, pearls
    and no dinner invitations. Days full of nobody's stories but my own.
You talk about *Flygirl*, your screenplay, over dinner so you can
    write our dates off on your taxes.
You're fighting with the waiter, sending back your burger, insisting,
    Make it new, don't just scrape the ketchup off.

And yet weren't we happy for awhile? Maybe even tender? Remember
this night: coming to bed, I hurry past the window's cold lens,
and you say, *Wait. This is the best part: you, naked, in the light,* and I hover

a moment like an unsure moth.
Now, if you still want to,

                                                                CUT TO

the rewrite that follows every break-up. Go ahead.
Make me the villainess. Make plot point one cruelty, not love.
Give me a new part. I'll be the girl on the tarmac leaving,
but without peace in mind, without the promise of a city
we'll always call ours. Gone is the jazz piano. And the blue smell of rain.
It's 74 degrees in LA, the city where nothing changes. There I am,
open lips but faraway, the propeller's shadow raking light
and darkness through me. Call me tease. Call us doomed to FADE OUT.

Secrets the Whales Wish They Didn't Know

Don't be surprised if ten years from now
that Karmann Ghia you've always wanted — sea-foam green,
black leather interior — shows up in your driveway
with a note from me and you remember
that summer of a thousand identical parties
when I claimed to love everyone, posing
with the neck of a Killian's in one fist;
in the other, your unfinished heart.

All talk, no action, you accused, leaning
on the iron fence at the Oldest Trick Café, downing
your third shot-in-the-dark. I didn't tell you
how long I had lived at the bottom of the sea
with the big slow lurking fish, how afraid I was
I might drown you. Which is why
late that night in the arms of the great magnolia —
when you called me *tiger* and blamed the tilt of the world
on the unlit stars between us — the leaves, green hearts,
that seemed to say, *Press your lives together*, I refused
to climb after you, but instead dangled my legs
from the bottom branches and warned,
if you touched them, the white of the petals would brown.

I was always a defender of beauty, you see:
your unlocked doors and easy sleep. I would do anything
to keep you wild and willing, to spare you
the secrets of the whales who swim from shipwreck
to shipwreck, studying the ghosts
of sailors who braved the wrong storms.

Girls Who Will Never Be Prom Queens

It's the night before her prom and Mariah's cousin models her dress
out in the garden, spinning between the foxglove and calla lilies
to show the younger kids how her skirt flares out
in a lacy cloud about her thighs.
She isn't thin. You might even say she's plump,
but plump, despite its dull drop from the tongue,
can be beautiful. Plump can be the memory of a carnation
corsage or peach juice dripping down the chin. And sometimes
it's a girl in white who loves herself and her dress and the way
her thick blonde braid is whipping out behind her.

The twelve-year-old boys on the grass
seem to know this, too, as they lay their heads
next to the gardenia's bottom blooms, the scent of which
will forever remind them — even when they are old married men
who have touched their wives everywhere — of this night,
of this twirling girl at twilight whose giggle is a string of pearls,
whose confidence leans like a ladder into the sky.

The other girls in the garden, Mariah's little sister
and her best friend with the cleft palate scar,
are just as mesmerized, chins in their palms, elbows in the wormy soil,
thinking one day it will be them by the butterfly bushes
practicing a slow dance, wetting their lips in the moonlight, ready
to say yes to the promises they can sense forming even now
in the boys like the first green glow of shoots
breaking the sheaths of seeds.
They take their eyes off the spinning girl just for a moment,
just to make sure the smooth-chinned, bony boys
are watching. And even though the girls aren't equipped
to distinguish between loving a girl in a prom dress
and falling in love with love, jealousy doesn't tap its egg
tooth on the dome of this evening. Young enough

still to be conscious of the bra straps across their backs,
they imagine, as the breeze lifts the dancing girl's skirt
even higher, the feel of a prom king's fingertips
unhooking the clasp. They think it's the perfumed wind
giving them goosebumps all over. They think
if true love doesn't find them soon they will die.

Me? I know we're not diamonds awaiting discovery.
We are dumb fluttery girls. One day our song
wakes the birds and outlasts the frogs' evening percussion.
The next morning, we can't find that love anywhere.
We search for it like misplaced keys. When we walk away
we slink against the night. I want to go outside to the garden
and tell the little girls the truth: that there is no truth.
I want to show them how Mariah's tears
have stiffened the skin of my palms. *Love is not bluebells
and tadpoles*, I will tell them. *It's not even the sweet
bloom of heartache. One day you'll look up and see
the stars are not windows. They're blisters on the sky.*

But it wouldn't matter. I could show them my half-rose tattoo
that used to be initials; or Tony in my rearview mirror,
straddling the middle of the highway, a question getting smaller;
or Mariah who left her fiancé last week and locked herself
in the bathroom tonight after accidentally kissing me.
I could show them wrong hands
that feel just like the right ones, broken
guitar strings and wet pillowcases and the faces of exes
passed years later in bank lines and produce aisles.
Still those little girls by the marigolds would insist on falling in love.
And I can't help wishing I, too, could put on a silk dress
and join the scene below. But I'm afraid that the minute I thrust

my sharp beak of a heart into that garden
all the soft backs of the rabbits would bristle, the drunken bumble bees
would drop from the air underside-up, the snapdragons bend
toward the weeds. And the dancing girl, the dancing girl would stop.

Instructions on How to Leave Me

Tell me again about that dream where,
in my lace skirt, I'm stealing your blueberries
faster than you pick them. Tell me how that day

for decades has spread its sweet dark stain
inside you. Remind me of our feet swinging
from the church pew, good shoes knocking together.

Any old memory will do: my Indian-head nickel
flattened on the train tracks, the bad
haircut I got to match yours, you winning me

the onionskin marble from Rush the Crusher.
Or our panic every time we couldn't find
Bob, your dad's retired firedog

that Crazy Miss Robins used to take into town
without asking, letting him ride shotgun,
buying him cheeseburgers at the drive-thru.

Tell me the stories the grown-ups told on porches
as they shelled peas and we organized
our army men, adding up our casualties

in little piles of pewter soldiers. Kiss me
the way you did that first time
in Dr. Harper's office after hours as we waited

for your mother to come out crying with the news,
so sure we were the snake was poisonous
and you were going to die. Kiss me like that,

as if to say you're sorry you're about to leave, sorry
for the unpartnered square dances, ungiven presents
of kittens and decoder rings, undedicated

late-night radio songs. No. Don't
say anything. Just look at me the way you did
that first time you thought you had to go. And go.

Last Word

At sixteen I come to the ledge again.
There is nothing between the sky and me
but so much between my body
and the ground: windows I would pass on the way
down, businessmen distracted from their phone calls by
a blur they wouldn't know was me until
the sirens came to still the typing fingers, stop
the herd of morning traffic, remind the city
of its children who might not be in school.

This is for Matt Parker who called me fat
in seventh grade, for the doctor who said I'd always fall
below the growth curve, for the saccharinely pretty
girl who stole my seat in calculus, for Mom and Dad
who made us give up the dog rather than build
a fence. This is for the cop who caught me
speeding, the postman who comes empty-handed, for the rumor-
starters and the Taco Bell woman
who never smiles or gives the right change.

But mostly, here with my arms outstretched, pretending
to dare the wind to take me, I'm an alarm
wailing in the night, set off by a banging
shutter, waking the house for nothing. My bandages
and blades are not well-hidden, journals earmarked
at warning passages and left open. I cry,
leaning against the thin walls
and still my family sleeps. I tore down
my posters, burned my dolls. No one asks why.

Maybe it takes an actual jump: the sound

of my life briefly on the wind. Maybe to see me
they have to kneel by my body like a test
someone finally scored incorrect;
they have to close the zeroes of my eyes.
Tomorrow I will come back and do this again.
But not today. I don't really want to be a concrete
signature. I want to grow old choosing ink over blood
with which, on the flank of the world, I'll set my brand.

The Streets of My Heart
for Jeff

What a display. The light chromed off the ornate lamps and signs,
brass bumpers of the Cadillac Sevilles,
spatulas sterling-gripped and forks gold-tined
that swung from every balcony's smoking grill.
Girls half-undressed came masquerading, frills
on sale to the debonair boys. Parading lines
of pigeons, curbside, puffed like helium-filled
balloons no one saw deflating. The shine
must fade, the city still, to gleam, to escapade anew.
The streets of my heart while sun-licked, well-trafficked, amazed,
hosted a previous traveler or two. But none until you
paused to point out beauty I missed: loves taxiing away;
the saxist on Oak, case open for coins, blue kiss at high noon;
jay-filled sapling in a slip of leaves, some stenciled to the walk by rain.

Sonogram on the Way to Earth

One of only two unpregnant at the baby shower, I offer
my chair to a globe-bellied one, fetch water
for another who has just begun to show.
I'll be in charge of the trash, I volunteer, collecting pastel
wrappings and ribbons, keeping busy, keeping quiet
about the fact that Jeff and I, for the better
part of a year, have been trying to start
a life inside me, too. I quell an image
of my reproductive system as an engine refusing
to crank. *Think positively,* I remind myself, and listen
to the symptom talk, labor jitters, the word *sonogram,*

which sounds to me like a character in a science
fiction novel, an alien on its way
across the galaxy, earthbound, his ship another blip
among the static of the stars; an alien
whose home awaits him as he marvels
at how opposite of void space is,
even the light years between planets riddled
with small wonders: asteroid belts
and the occasional drifting debris
from ships that didn't make it. His eyes bounce back
from the stratosphere to the map of Earth
he's pinned to the oxygen tank. He's expectant,

like me, though my belly's as flat as the ancients misconceived
the world to be, not knowing that on one lucky morning
breeze, one of their bravest
would meet the horizon and fail to drop
off. One of the shower moms gasps, surprised
by her baby's kick, his strongest yet, as if he's anxious
to get moving. And me, the not-yet-Mom
holding the garbage bag, I smile wider

than all the rest as I picture my Sonogram
practicing for the moment his vessel arrives, the kick
that will open the hatch.

Heart by Heart the House

       will empty, thread by thread all hems
unstitch.
       Not even the twin oaks will last, though their roots
       insist themselves,
           buckling the limestone

       drive. Tonight you fly,
           above your head, our arthritic cat who has lived
too long to protest, who will probably be the next
           to go. I am trying
       not to cling. I am trying

           to remember the look
       flooding your father's face that
morning he discovered tomatoes destroyed
       despite his careful fencing. What could he do
           but plant again
       in the furnace of a new day's heat, thinking
       of your mother cooking, that very minute, corn
gleaned yesterday from his garden? Maybe

       we'll bring into this world five children and ruin
       every one, regardless of inoculations, safety belts,
       Tot-Finder decals silver
in their windows — that may serve no purpose
       but to remind them to be afraid of fire, my own
       childhood fear — flames
       raking the irreplaceable — with me still
but disappearing. Sometimes — even
       as cell by cell we're breaking, even
       as my mind, more sieve than cup, lets go of you, lets go — I

       am overtaken by a moment's calm, relieved

not to know what's coming. Do I want us
to die at the same time and turn
into trees or start over
as ourselves: our first
encounter, kiss, our great mistakes
ahead